I Like Weather!

Why Is It Snowing?

Judith Williams

Enslow Elementary
an imprint of

E **Enslow Publishers, Inc.**

40 Industrial Road   PO Box 38
Box 398   Aldershot
Berkeley Heights, NJ 07922   Hants GU12 6BP
USA   UK

http://www.enslow.com

Words to Know

blizzard (BLIH zurd)—Cold weather with strong winds and blowing snow.

snow crystal (KRIH stuhl)—Water vapor that turns into ice.

snowflake (SNOH flayk)—Snow crystals that are stuck together and fall from the sky.

water cycle (SY kul)—The movement of water from the earth, into the sky, and back to earth again.

water vapor (VAY pur)—Water that has turned from liquid into a gas, such as fog.

Contents

Where does snow start? 4

How does water vapor become snow? 6

How many shapes can snow crystals have? 8

How do snow crystals become snowflakes? 10

Why are some snowflakes so big? 12

What is a blizzard? 14

How can you measure snow? 16

Why is snow important? 18

Experiment 20

Learn More
 Books 22
 Web Sites 23

Index 24

Where does snow start?

Snow is part of Earth's water cycle.

First the sun heats the water on Earth—in the land, rivers, and oceans.

The heat turns some of the water into a gas. This gas is called water vapor.

The vapor rises into the sky.

Water vapor rises.

Ocean

Land

How does water vapor become snow?

When the air is very cold, the vapor turns into tiny pieces of ice. The ice pieces are called snow crystals. When there are enough snow crystals, they form a cloud.

Snow Crystals

How many shapes can snow crystals have?

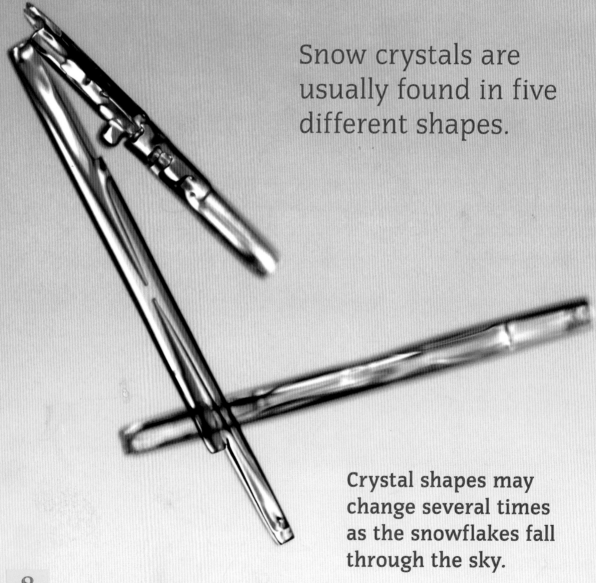

Snow crystals are usually found in five different shapes.

Crystal shapes may change several times as the snowflakes fall through the sky.

Colder air makes crystals with fancy shapes. Warmer air makes crystals with simpler shapes. All snow crystals have six sides.

How do snow crystals become snowflakes?

The snow crystals move around in the clouds. The snow crystals bump into other snow crystals. The crystals stick together.

When the crystals are heavy enough, they fall to the ground. We call them snowflakes!

Snow crystals may melt and freeze many times before landing.

Why are some snowflakes so big?

Big snowflakes are a bunch of small flakes stuck together. Flakes stick together in warmer winter air. Big snowflakes do not usually fall if it is very cold or windy.

Warmer winter air often makes sticky snow—perfect for making snowballs and snowmen!

What is a blizzard?

A blizzard is unsafe winter weather.
Lots of snow falls, and the air gets very cold.
Strong winds blow the snow really hard.

It is hard to see in a blizzard.
Traveling is not safe.

How can you measure snow?

Stand a ruler in the snow to measure how much snow has fallen.

A high amount of snow can make driving unsafe. Schools can close. Airports can shut down.

Why is snow important?

Melting snow gives water back to the land, rivers, and oceans. Then the water cycle can start over. Someday, the water may become a snowflake again.

But when snow is still frozen, playing outside is lots of fun!

What takes up more space, snow or water?

You will need:

- ❖ 1 jar or glass
- ❖ snow, or crushed ice from a snow cone

1. Fill a jar or glass to the top with snow or crushed ice. Do not pack the snow.

2. Leave the jar on a counter until all the snow has melted. Is the jar still full?

Snowflakes do not fit together tightly. There are spaces between the snowflakes. The spaces are filled with air. When the snow melts, the air spaces are gone.

Water does not have air spaces, so it takes up less space than snow.

Fun fact: You get about one inch of water from twelve inches of snow.

Learn More

Books

Ashwell, Miranda, and Andy Owen. *Snow*. Des Plaines, Ill.: Heinemann Library, 1999.

Branley, Franklyn M. *Snow Is Falling*. New York: HarperTrophy, 2000.

Waldman, Neil. *The Snowflake: A Water Cycle Story*. Brookfield, Conn.: Millbrook Press, 2003.

Web Sites

Make a Flake
http://snowflakes.lookandfeel.com/

FEMA for Kids: Winter Storms
http://www.fema.gov/kids/wntstrm.htm

National Geographic
http://news.nationalgeographic.com/news/2004/02/
photogalleries/snowflakes/

Index

air, 6, 8, 12, 14, 21
airports, 16
blizzard, 14
cloud, 6, 10
Earth, 4
ice, 6
school, 16

snow, 4, 6, 14, 20, 21
measuring, 16
melting, 18, 20–21
snow crystals, 6, 7, 8–9
shape, 10–11
snowflakes, 11, 18, 21
size, 12

sun, 4
water, 20, 21
water cycle, 4, 18
water vapor, 4, 5, 6
winds, 14

Enslow Elementary, an imprint of Enslow Publishers, Inc.

Enslow Elementary® is a registered trademark of Enslow Publishers, Inc.

Copyright © 2005 by Enslow Publishers, Inc.

All rights reserved.

No part of this book may be reproduced by any means without the written permission of the publisher.

Library of Congress Cataloging-in-Publication Data

Williams, Judith (Judith A.)
    Why is it snowing? / Judith Williams.
        p. cm. — (I like weather!)
    Includes bibliographical references and index.
    ISBN 0-7660-2319-2
    1. Snow—Juvenile literature. I. Title.
    QC926.37.W55 2005
    551.57'84—dc22

                                        2004016790

Printed in the United States of America

10 9 8 7 6 5 4 3 2 1

To Our Readers: We have done our best to make sure all Internet Addresses in this book were active and appropriate when we went to press. However, the author and the publisher have no control over and assume no liability for the material available on those Internet sites or on other Web sites they may link to. Any comments or suggestions can be sent by e-mail to comments@enslow.com or to the address on the back cover.

Photo Credits: AP/Wide World, p. 16; © 2004 JupiterImages, pp. 6, 13, 19; © 2004 Michael DeYoung/AlaskaStock.com, p. 15; Dr. Jeremy Burgess/Science Photo Library, p. 8; Jim W. Grace/Photo Researchers, Inc., p. 12; © Ken Redding/CORBIS, p. 18; Photos by Ken Libbrecht, pp. 7, 10–11; © Rommel/Masterfile, p. 9; © Scott Tysick/Masterfile, p. 17; Tom LaBaff, p. 5.

Cover Photo: © 2004 Alaska Stock LLC

Every effort has been made to locate all copyright holders of material used in this book. If any errors or omissions have occurred, corrections will be made in future editions of this book.

Series Literacy Consultant

Allan A. De Fina, Ph.D.
Past President of the
New Jersey Reading Association
Professor, Department of
Literacy Education
New Jersey City University

Science Consultant

Harold Brooks, Ph.D.
NOAA/National Severe
Storms Laboratory
Norman, Oklahoma

Note to Parents and Teachers:
The **I Like Weather!** series supports the National Science Education Standards for K–4 science. The Words to Know section introduces subject-specific vocabulary words, including pronunciation and definitions. Early readers may need help with these new words.

24

J
551.5
W

JAN   2006

Williams, Judith

Why is it Snowing?

$15.95